WORLD RELIGIONS

FACTS ABOUT

BUDDHISM

Alison Cooper

New York

Published in 2011 by The Rosen Publishing Group Inc.
29 East 21st Street, New York, NY 10010

First Edition

Original designer and illustrator: Celia Hart
Layout for this edition: Jane Hawkins
Consultant: The Clear Vision Trust

Library of Congress Cataloging-in-Publication Data

Cooper, Alison, 1967-
 Facts about Buddhism / Alison Cooper.
    p. cm. — (World religions)
Includes index.
ISBN 978-1-61532-319-7 (library binding)
ISBN 978-1-61532-330-2 (paperback)
ISBN 978-1-61532-331-9 (6-pack)
1. Buddhism—Juvenile literature. I. Title.
BQ4032.C66 2011
294.3—dc22

                                2009052448

Photographs:
Bridgeman Art Library, p. 18 (The Mandala of Shasrabhuja
Avalokitesvara, Tunhuang, 9th century, Indochinese, National Museum
of India, New Delhi); British Museum, p16; British Library, p. 33(b);
Britstock, p. 32 (Bernd Ducke); Cephas, p. 26(t) (Nigel Blythe); Clear
Vision, p. 22(r); Patrick G. Cockell, p. 9; James Davis Travel
Photography, pp. 8(b), 21(b), 25(b), 27; Eye Ubiquitous pp. 21(tr),
23 (P.M. Field), 29(b) (John Hulme), 35(l) David Cumming, 35(br)
(Bennett Dean), 36(Tim Page); Robert Harding Picture Library, pp.
25(t), 28, 29(t), 31(b), 41(b) (Maurice Joseph); Michael Holford,
pp. 13(t), 15(t), 20; The Hutchison Library, pp. 17(t) (Sarah
Etherington), 19(l) (R. Ian Lloyd), 21 (tl) (Patricia Govcoolea),
37(b) (John Burbank); The Image Bank, p. 8(t) (Guido A. Rossi);
The Independent, p. 17(b); Magnum Photos, p. 13(b) (Chris Steel-
Perkins); Bipinchandra J. Mistry, pp. 19(r), 22(l), 40; Zul Mukhida,
pp. 24, 37(t); Christine Osborne Pictures, pp. 15(b), 26(b); Panos Pictures,
pp. 30 (Cliff Venner), 31(t) & 38 (Jean-Leo Dugart), 39(b) (Martin
Flitman), 41(t) (Neil Cooper); Bury Peerless, p. 12; Frank Spooner
Pictures, pp. 33(t) (Erik Sampers), 39(t); Spectrum Colour Library,
p35(tr) (W.R. Davis); Tantra Designs, endpapers (Peter Douglas) & p. 14.

Endpapers: A Tibetan lotus, the traditional Buddhist
symbol of Enlightenment (see page 16).

Manufactured in China
CPSIA Compliance Information: Batch #WAS0102YA: For Further Information
contact Rosen Publishing, New York, New York at 1-800-237-9932

CONTENTS

WHO ARE THE BUDDHISTS?

Buddhists are people who follow the teachings of a man named Siddhartha Gautama, who lived in India nearly 2,500 years ago. He spent many years trying to understand what made people unhappy and how they could find happiness. When he finally found the answers to his questions, he became known as the Buddha, which means "the Enlightened one." Buddhists use his teachings to guide them in their daily lives, toward enlightenment.

Monks and Nuns ▼

Some Buddhists give up their possessions and their family life in order to become monk or nuns. They spend their lives studying the holy books learning to meditate, and teaching. In some Buddhist countries, young boys spend time in a monastery as part of their education. The boys below are studying in Thailand. They are wearing traditional orange robes.

▲ A Stupa

A stupa is a sacred place for Buddhists. Stupas are often built as places to keep holy books or relics (see page 24). Sometimes, they are built to mark a special place in Buddhist history. The photograph above shows the stupa of Bodhnath in Kathmandu, Nepal. The eyes of the Buddha are painted on all four sides of the spire, to show that the Buddha sees everything in the world around him.

Canada
United States
Brazil

United Kingdom
France
Italy
Germany
Kalmykia
Russian Federation
Tyva
Buryatia
Mongolia
North & South Korea
Japan
China
Nepal
Bhutan
Tibet
India
Burma
Taiwan
Hong Kong
Laos
Vietnam
Cambodia
Sri Lanka
Thailand
Malaysia
Singapore
Indonesia
Australia
New Zealand

Estimated Buddhist population:

Over 10 million

1 to 10 million

100,000 to 1 million

5,000 to 100,000

NUMBERS OF BUDDHISTS

There are probably about 400 million Buddhists around the world. In the United States, they make up less than one percent of the population, but in some Asian countries, such as Thailand, almost the entire population is Buddhist.

The Buddhist World ▶

After the Buddha's death, his followers split into two main groups. Mahayana Buddhists spread the Buddha's teachings into China, Vietnam, Korea, Japan, Nepal, Tibet, and Mongolia. Theravada Buddhists spread his teaching into Sri Lanka, Burma, Thailand, and other parts of Southeast Asia. Since the early twentieth century, there have been Buddhist communities in Europe and the U.S.A. The pagoda on the right was built in London by Japanese Buddhists in 1985.

TIMELINE

THE DEVELOPMENT OF BUDDHISM

B.C.E. = Before the Common Era = B.C. (term used by Christians)

C.E. = in the time of the Common Era = A.D. (term used by Christians)

C. 480 B.C.E.	C. 445 B.C.E.	C. 400 B.C.E.	400–314 B.C.E.	268–239 B.C.E.
Siddhartha Gautama is born at Lumbini in Nepal. At the age of 29, he leaves his father's palace to begin his search for the meaning of life.	Gautama gains enlightenment and becomes the Buddha.	Death of the Buddha. His followers travel through Asia, spreading his teachings.	Two councils are held to collect the Buddha's teachings together. Different ways of practicing Buddhism develop, including Theravada Buddhism.	Reign of Emperor Ashoka Maurya in India. He becomes a Buddhist after seeing thousands killed in battle.

Siddhartha Gautama, the Buddha

1642 C.E.	1197 C.E.	1191 C.E.	TWELFTH CENTURY C.E.	630–645 C.E.
The fifth Dalai Lama becomes the religious and political leader of Tibet.	The great Buddhist university of Nalanda in India is destroyed by Muslims.	Zen Buddhism is introduced into Japan from China.	Hinduism and Islam have become the major religions in India—Buddhism almost disappears.	The Chinese monk, Hsuan Tsang, visits Buddhist sites in India.
1643 C.E. The Potala Palace is built in Lhasa, Tibet, as the Dalai Lama's winter home.				

▲ The Potala Palace, Lhasa

Statue from Jokhang Temple, Tibet ▲

1881 C.E.	1891 C.E.	1907 C.E.	1930 C.E.	1935 C.E.
The Pali Text Society is set up to translate and publish Pali writings into European languages.	The Mahabodhi Society is founded in Sri Lanka. It seeks to raise money to restore the sacred Buddhist sites in India.	The first Buddhist society in the UK is founded.	The Buddhist Society of America is formed.	Birth of Tenzin Gyatso, the 14th and present Dalai Lama, leader of the Tibetan Buddhists.

Emperor Ashoka

In 259 B.C.E., Emperor Ashoka Maurya attacked Kalinga on the east coast of India. This was one of the few areas of India that was not part of his empire. Although Ashoka won the battle, 100,000 people were killed in the fighting and thousands more were wounded. Ashoka was so upset and ashamed that he decided to become a Buddhist. From then on, he tried to follow the Buddhist teachings about kindness and nonviolence.

C. 250 B.C.E.
Ashoka's son and daughter spread the Buddha's teachings to Sri Lanka. Missionaries also travel to Burma and Thailand.

80 B.C.E.
The Pali Canon is written down for the first time, in Sri Lanka.

100 B.C.E.– 100 C.E.
Mahayana Buddhism develops. Buddhism spreads to China.

The lion-headed top from a pillar inscribed with the story of Ashoka. ▶

100 C.E.– 200 C.E.
The first images of the Buddha are made. Before this, the Buddha was shown in symbols.

C. 642 C.E.
Buddhism spreads to Tibet.

C. 538 C.E.
Buddhism spreads to Japan.

C. 372 C.E.
Buddhism spreads to Korea.

▲ The wheel is an important Buddhist symbol. It appears on the flag of India.

Buddhism in Tibet

The Dalai Lamas ruled Tibet and were the religious leaders of Tibet's Buddhists from 1642 to 1951. In 1951, the Chinese army invaded and in 1959, the Dalai Lama was forced to leave. The Chinese invaders were Communists who were against all religious beliefs. They destroyed Buddhist monasteries. Thousands of monks were arrested and killed. From India, the Dalai Lama led a long campaign for a free Tibet.

◀ Tenzin Gyatso, the 14th Dalai Lama

1967 C.E.
The Friends of the Western Buddhist Order is set up. The movement combines Theravada, Tibetan, and Zen traditions.

1989 C.E.
The Dalai Lama is awarded the Nobel Peace Prize.

2004 C.E.
The Dalai Lama continues efforts to negotiate with the Chinese government and win freedom for Tibet.

HOW DID BUDDHISM BEGIN?

Buddhism began around 2,500 years ago. Its founder, Siddhartha Gautama, was the son of an Indian nobleman. When he was born, a wise man said that he would become either a great ruler or a great holy man. Gautama's father wanted his son to rule after him, and he tried to keep him away from the outside world. He did everything he could to make his son happy. Gautama married his beautiful cousin, Yashodara, and they had a son, named Rahula.

▲ The Four Sights

One day, Gautama went riding in his chariot outside the palace walls. He saw an old man, a sick man, and a dead man, and was shocked to see so much suffering. His chariot driver explained that old age, sickness, and death come to everyone eventually. Finally, Gautama saw a holy man, who was poor, yet happy and contented.

USEFUL WORDS

Buddha—The "Enlightened" or "Awakened One."
Dharma—The teachings of the Buddha and the way people follow them in their daily lives.
Nirvana—The state of perfect happiness reached by people who have achieved enlightenment.
Enlightenment—Achieving enlightenment is like waking from a dream and seeing things as they really are.

A Hard Life ▼

That night Gautama left the palace. He spent six hard years living in the forest. He starved himself to clear his mind and understand the truth about life.

The starving Buddha

◄ Becoming the Buddha

While meditating in the shade of a tree one day, Gautama realized that starving did not make his mind clearer. He understood that people are unhappy because they are never content with what they have. He also saw a way out of this. He had achieved Enlightenment. From then on, he became known as the Buddha, the "Enlightened," or "Awakened one."

◄ Life and Death

The Buddha spent the rest of his life traveling around India, teaching people freedom from suffering. He died at the age of 80. This statue shows him lying on his side at his death. Buddhists describe his death as parinirvana, meaning that his work was done and he could enter the final nirvana.

WHAT DID THE BUDDHA TEACH?

The Buddha knew that neither great luxury nor great hardship brought happiness. He taught people to follow a Middle Path between these two extremes. By doing this, they could overcome greed and desire, and lead wiser, more caring lives. He also taught that each person had to find the truth for himself or herself. His teachings—called the Dharma—were a guide to help them.

The Wheel of Life ▲

The Wheel of Life, shown above, is a very important symbol for Buddhists. It represents the cycle of birth, death, and rebirth, which is always turning, like a wheel. The outer circle shows the stages of a person's life. The middle circle shows different ways in which you might be reborn. In the center are three animals that stand for hatred, greed, and confusion. These prevent people achieving Enlightenment.

THE NOBLE EIGHTFOLD PATH

The Middle Path is also called the Noble Eightfold Path. The spokes of the Dharma-wheel represent the eight steps of the path, which all have to work together.

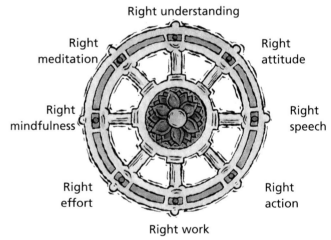

Right understanding
Right meditation
Right attitude
Right mindfulness
Right speech
Right effort
Right action
Right work

Right understanding—of the Buddha's teaching
Right attitude—following the Buddha's path
Right speech—speaking kindly and truthfully
Right action—not harming any person or animal
Right work—which does not make others suffer
Right effort—thinking kindly and positively
Right mindfulness— aware of self and others
Right meditation—for a calm, wise mind

▲ The Buddha Begins Teaching

The painting above shows the Buddha teaching in the countryside. The Buddha gave his first talk at Sarnath in India and soon gained many followers. The Buddha spent the next 45 years as a monk, traveling and spreading his message.

Teaching Today ▶

After the Buddha's death, his followers continued his teachings. Teaching and studying the Dharma are still important today. These boys in Sri Lanka are studying at a monastery. They learn about Buddhism as well as their other school subjects. Some students become monks but others return to their families.

WHAT ELSE DO BUDDHISTS BELIEVE?

Buddhists believe in the teaching of karma. This is that kind actions bring a person closer to nirvana, or Enlightenment—a state of perfect happiness. Unkind actions hold you back from Enlightenment. Being born as a human is a great opportunity to develop qualities such as loving kindness, calmness, and generosity. These help people to achieve true happiness. Everyone has the strength within themselves to change their behavior and lead more fulfilling, happier lives.

The Three Jewels ▶

The three wheels in the picture represent the Three Jewels of Buddhism. These are the Buddha himself, the Dharma, and the Buddhist community, which is called the Sangha. They are called the Three Jewels because they are so precious. When a person becomes a Buddhist, they try to put Three Jewels at the center of their life.

Lotus flowers

▲ Lotus Flowers

Lotus flowers have their roots in muddy ponds but they grow toward the light. They are a symbol of the Buddhist belief that people can change and move toward enlightenment.

THE THREE FIRES

The Three Fires are hatred, greed, and ignorance, which prevent a person from achieving nirvana. Chanting the sacred texts, meditating, and helping other people all help to damp down the flames. When the Three Fires have been completely put out, the person has achieved nirvana.

◄ The Sangha

The Sangha, or Buddhist community, is made up of monks, nuns, and ordinary people. Helping others is an essential part of belonging to the Sangha. Through helping others, people become less greedy and selfish, and learn to share whatever they have. One way for monks to help people is by passing on the teachings of the Buddha. The monks in this picture are blessing a crowd of worshipers in Bhutan.

Caring for the Earth ►

Buddhists believe that everything has an effect on other things. They try not to cause pollution or to destroy living things. The Buddhists in the photograph on the right are working to produce all the food they need for their own community, without harming the earth.

DOES BUDDHISM HAVE ANY GODS?

Buddhists do not believe in an all-powerful God who created the world and watches over it. They worship the Buddha as a human being who achieved Enlightenment. By living by his teachings, people have the opportunity to achieve Enlightenment for themselves. Buddhists believe that there were buddhas before Siddhartha Gautama and that there are other buddhas still to come.

◀ Bodhisattvas

A bodhisattva is a mythical being who has dedicated his or her life to helping all living beings free themselves from suffering. Mahayana Buddhists try to become like them. The picture shows Avalokiteshvara, a bodhisattva worshiped for his great loving kindness.

QUESTIONING IDEAS

The Buddha did not want people to accept everything he said without question, as though he were God. Instead, they should try his teachings out and see if they work.

18

Green Tara ▶

This painting on the right shows a bodhisattva named Green Tara. One legend says that she was born from a lotus that blossomed from Avalokiteshvara's tears of compassion. She, too, is worshiped for the great care she shows to people who are unhappy or suffering.

The Buddha to Come ▶

The picture on the right shows Maitreya, who will be the next Buddha. Presently, he lives in one of the many Buddhist heavens but when he comes to earth, life will be better and it will be easier to achieve Enlightenment.

Maitreya

Golden Buddhas ▲

The photograph above shows some of the golden statues of the Buddha in a temple named Wat Po in Thailand (*Wat* is the Thai word for "temple"). There are 394 statues in the row altogether. Images of the Buddha remind worshipers that they are capable of achieving Enlightenment, just as the Buddha did.

ARE THERE DIFFERENT GROUPS OF BUDDHISTS?

All Buddhists share the same basic beliefs in the Three Jewels, but they have different ways of understanding the Buddha's teaching and of practicing their faith. The two main groups are Theravada Buddhists and Mahayana Buddhists. Theravada Buddhists believe that the Buddha alone helps them. Mahayana Buddhists also believe in "heavenly" buddhas and bodhisattvas who teach people and listen to their prayers.

Zen Buddhism ▼

Zen Buddhism is a type of Mahayana Buddhism. It is practiced mainly in China and Japan. Zen Buddhists aim to achieve Enlightenment through meditation. They use poetry and paintings to help them to focus their mind. A frog is shown in the painting below because frogs are admired for their stillness and watchfulness.

A Zen painting

Pure Land Buddhists ▲

Pure Land Buddhism is a type of Mahayana Buddhism that is popular in China and Japan. Its followers worship Amitabha, the buddha of infinite light (shown above). They believe they will go to his Pure Land when they die, and so move closer to nirvana.

▲ Zen Monks

These Zen monks are about to set out on a journey to a sacred site. They are wearing traveling clothes—black robes and white trousers, with straw hats and sandals. Many Zen monasteries have a sand garden (above right). The peaceful atmosphere helps the monks to meditate.

Tibetan Buddhism ▶

Buddhism came to Tibet from India in the eighth century C.E. Tibetan Buddhists follow the Mahayana teachings. The photograph shows the Sera monastery, which was built in 1419 C.E. It became a great center of learning and meditation. But many of its sacred books and paintings were destroyed by the Chinese after they invaded Tibet in 1951.

HOW DO BUDDHISTS LIVE?

Buddhists have five guidelines, called the Five Precepts (see opposite page). They try to keep to these guidelines as they go about their daily lives.

The Buddha told people that only when they understood themselves could they really help other people. If people want to become kinder and wiser, then they need to develop more awareness.

Meditation ▶

This Western Buddhist is meditating. Meditation is very important for Buddhists and many Buddhists meditate every day. They sit cross-legged or in a chair, close their eyes, and breathe calmly and evenly.

Buddhists meditate because they believe that training their minds to be still will help them to understand themselves better and move closer to Enlightenment. Some focus on an object, such as a candle, which helps them to relax. Others use chants to help them to concentrate.

◀ Counting Beads

Some Buddhists use a *mala* like the one on the left to help them to meditate. As they touch each bead, they chant the name of the Buddha or a bodhisattva, or they say a sacred word or phrase, called a mantra.

A mandala

Mandalas ▲

Tibetan Buddhists use circular pictures called mandalas to help them to meditate. In the center, there is an image that represents a quality, such as wisdom. There are four openings around it. These are doorways you can go through to reach the quality in the center. The different colors represent different qualities, too. For example, red stands for the Buddha's warmth and loving kindness. White stands for his purity.

Burning Incense ▲

The woman in the photograph above is burning incense sticks in front of a huge statue of the Buddha. Incense has a sweet smell, which reminds people of the beauty of the Buddha's teaching. As the incense burns, the worshiper might say a chant.

WHERE DO BUDDHISTS WORSHIP?

Buddhists worship at home on their own, with a group, or in a temple or

monastery. They worship in front of a shrine. This contains an image of the Buddha or of a bodhisattva, surrounded by candles, flowers, and incense.

When the Buddha died, he was cremated and his ashes were taken to eight different places. Shrines called stupas were built over them. Later, Emperor Ashoka divided up the ashes again and put them in new stupas all over India. Other stupas hold relics of important monks and sacred texts.

◀ **A Shrine at Home**
This photograph shows a shrine in a family home in Sri Lanka. There are several statues of the Buddha, a lamp, and a packet of incense sticks. Each day, members of the family stand in front of the shrine and chant the Three Jewels and the Five Precepts.

STYLES OF STUPA

The first stupas were shaped like domes. Different styles developed as Buddhism spread to other countries.

1. Stupa (India) 2. Dagoba (Sri Lanka) 3. Chorten (Tibet) 4. Pagoda (China/Japan)

The Jokhang Temple ▶

The Jokhang Temple in Lhasa is the most important temple in Tibet. This photograph shows trays of lamps burning in the shrine. Lighting lamps or candles is an important part of Buddhist worship. The light that shines from them is a symbol of the wisdom that the Buddha's teaching brings.

◀ Shwedagon

The Shwedagon Pagoda in Burma is said to contain eight of the Buddha's hairs. It is one of the most sacred Buddhist sites. Its towers are covered in gold and decorated with precious stones.

Prayer Flags in Tibet ▶

Prayer flags flutter from Tibetan temples. Their verses of blessing are carried on the wind.

HOW DO BUDDHISTS WORSHIP?

There is no special day of the week for Buddhists to visit the temple, although festivals and full moon days are important times for worship. When the worshipers enter the temple, they clasp their hands together as a greeting. Then they kneel and bow three times before the statue of the Buddha or the bodhisattva in the shrine room. They make offerings and chant their faith in the Three Jewels. They might light incense or listen to a monk reading from the sacred texts.

◀ Inside the Temple
This photograph shows worshipers in the main shrine room of the Shwedagon Pagoda in Burma. They have taken off their shoes as a sign of respect.

Temple Offerings ▶
By making offerings like the ones in the photograph, people remember the Buddha's wise example. The sweet smell of incense stands for their belief that living kindly and wisely has a positive effect on the world. The flowers soon die, reminding people that nothing lasts forever. As well as symbolic offerings such as these, people leave gifts of food for the monks.

Prayer Wheels ▲

A prayer wheel is a cylinder with a scroll of paper inside it.
Thousands of mantras are written on the scroll. The
Tibetan woman in the picture is turning each prayer wheel
as she walks around the temple. By doing this, she releases
the blessings into the world. As she turns the wheels, she
chants a mantra.

Prayer wheel

Bell

Vajra

Tibetan Worship ▲

The prayer wheel shown above is carried
around and people spin it as they walk.
The bell is rung during religious ceremonies.
It symbolizes wisdom. The vajra is a symbol
of the Buddha's powerful wisdom.

WHO ARE THE BUDDHIST HOLY MEN AND WOMEN?

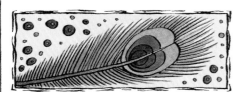

Some Buddhists choose to spend their lives practicing, studying, and teaching the Buddha's message, instead of having a family life. The Buddha himself lived like this, moving from place to place and relying on gifts of food from local people. Among his first companions were the five holy men who lived in the forest with the Buddha when he was seeking enlightenment, his son, Rahula, and his cousin, Ananda.

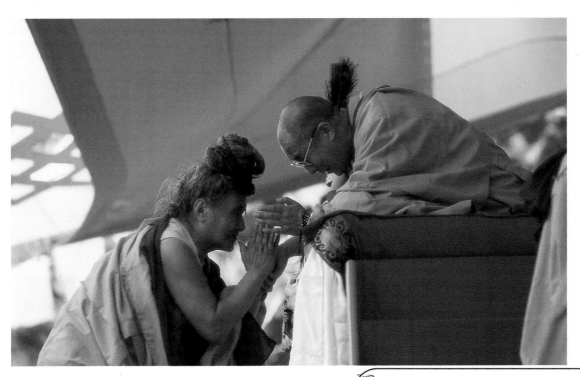

The Dalai Lama ▲

The Dalai Lama (above) is the leader of Tibet's Buddhists. His title means "a teacher whose wisdom is as deep as the ocean." Tibetans believe that the Dalai Lama is the bodhisattva named Avalokiteshvara, in human form.

THE FIRST MONKS

This is an extract from what the Buddha said when he sent out his followers to teach the Dharma:

"Go forth, O monks, for the joy and well-being of many, out of compassion for the world . . . Preach, O monks, the message which is noble in its beginning, in its middle, and in its end."

◀ Buddhist Nuns

These women (left) are taking part in a ceremony in the UK to become Buddhist nuns. Like monks, nuns live very simply and they have very few belongings of their own.

Giving Alms ▼

In countries that follow Theravada Buddhism, such as Thailand, monks rely on local people for their food. Some of the monks go out with their alms bowls each morning. People give them food, as the man in the photograph is doing. The monks share the food back in the monastery.

Alms bowl

Khata

Khatas ▲

A *khata* is a white scarf. In Tibet, khatas are given to monks and teachers to show respect. They are used instead of flowers, because there are few flowers in Tibet.

WHAT IS LIFE LIKE IN A BUDDHIST MONASTERY?

Monks and nuns follow a set of rules, called the *vinaya*. These include the Five Precepts (see page 23), which all Buddhists try to follow. The rules also say that they must not eat after noon, dance or sing just for fun, wear jewelry, sleep in a soft bed, or accept gifts of money. Monks and nuns spend their time studying the sacred texts, chanting, meditating, and running the monastery.

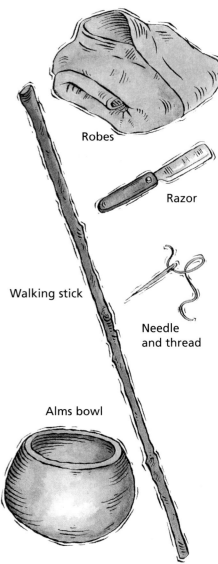

Robes

Razor

Walking stick

Needle and thread

Alms bowl

Sacred Dance ▲

These Tibetan monks are performing a sacred dance in the courtyard of their monastery. They are carrying offerings of white scarves called khatas (see page 29) and blowing very long trumpets. Ceremonies like this are held to celebrate festivals and special occasions. They were a common sight in Tibet before the Chinese invaded in 1951.

◀ Daily Meal

Theravada monks eat their first meal early in the morning and their second meal before noon. They do not eat again until the next day, although they can drink water or tea without milk or sugar. This simple lifestyle leaves more time for meditation and study.

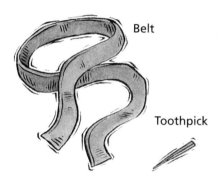

Belt

Toothpick

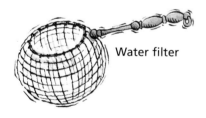

Water filter

 THE EIGHT REQUISITES

Traditionally, monks were only allowed to own eight items. You can see these in the illustration above. Their robes were saffron (an orange-yellow color), maroon, or black. They used the filter to make sure they did not accidentally swallow any living creatures in the water. Theravadin monks and nuns continue this tradition today.

▲ Work and Study

This Tibetan monk is cleaning pots and pans. Although monks help in the running of the monastery, they spend most of their time studying, chanting, and meditating. At the three biggest Tibetan monasteries, learned monks who have studied the sacred texts for 20 years or more are awarded a special degree.

WHICH ARE THE BUDDHIST SACRED TEXTS?

For more than 300 years after the Buddha's death, his followers learned his teachings by heart and passed them on from one generation to the next. In the first century B.C.E. his words were written down in an ancient language called Pali. These writings

became known as the Pali Canon and they are the sacred texts of all Buddhists, especially the Theravadins.

Mahayana Buddhists have different holy texts, which use stories to explain some of the Buddha's teachings.

◄ Making Books

As Buddhism spread into other countries, monks came to India from Tibet and China to copy the Buddha's teachings into their own language. They had to take great care over their work and it took many hours. Translating and copying the sacred texts still goes on today. These Tibetan monks are making books in their monastery library.

THE DHAMMAPADA

These are extracts from a collection of the Buddha's sayings, which is called the *Dhammapada*. It is part of the Pali Canon.

"If a man has faith and virtue, then
he has true glory and treasure.
Wherever that man may go,
There he will be held in honor."

"Conquer anger by love;
conquer evil by good;
conquer the mean by giving;
conquer the liar by truth."

"A thoughtless pilgrim only raises dust on the road."

The Three Baskets ▶

The Pali Canon is also called the Tripitaka, or Three Baskets. The first basket, or section, contains rules for monks and nuns to follow. The second contains the Dharma, or teaching, of the Buddha. The third basket contains writings that explain his teaching. These young monks are chanting from the sacred texts.

A Pali Text ▼

Some monks still read and chant the sacred texts in the ancient language, Pali.
This is an extract from the *Dhammapada*:

Sabba-papassa akaranam,
kusalassa upasampada
sa-citta-pariyodapanam
etam buddhana sasanam

Not to do any evil,
To cultivate the good,
To purify one's mind:
This is the teaching of the Buddhas.

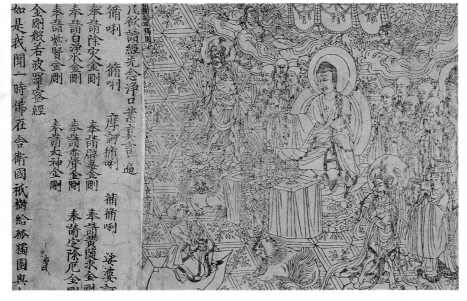

◀ The Sutras

The Mahayana sacred texts were first written in an ancient language called Sanskrit. Each section is called a sutra. The photograph on the left shows a page from the *Diamond Sutra*. This is one of the most important Mahayana texts and it is about Buddhist philosophy.

WHICH ARE THE BUDDHISTS' SACRED PLACES?

Some of the most sacred places for Buddhists are connected with events in the Buddha's life. One is Lumbini, in Nepal, where the Buddha was  born. Bodh Gaya, in India, is the place where he achieved Enlightenment and Sarnath is where he began his teaching. Kushinagara is the town where he died. Buddhists come from all over the world to visit sacred places such as these.

Sacred Places ▼
The map below shows some of the holiest places for Buddhists.

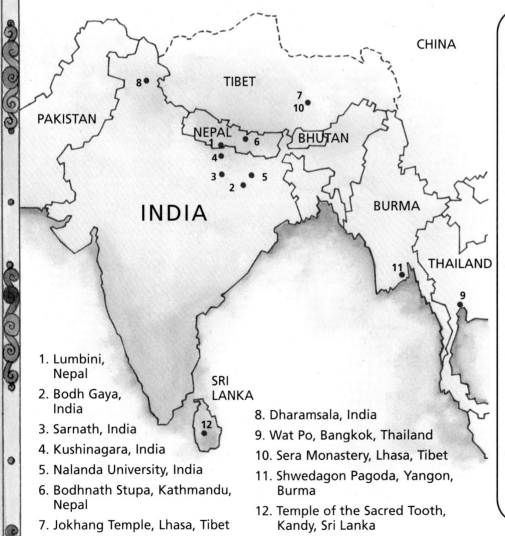

1. Lumbini, Nepal
2. Bodh Gaya, India
3. Sarnath, India
4. Kushinagara, India
5. Nalanda University, India
6. Bodhnath Stupa, Kathmandu, Nepal
7. Jokhang Temple, Lhasa, Tibet
8. Dharamsala, India
9. Wat Po, Bangkok, Thailand
10. Sera Monastery, Lhasa, Tibet
11. Shwedagon Pagoda, Yangon, Burma
12. Temple of the Sacred Tooth, Kandy, Sri Lanka

THE BUDDHA'S BIRTH

The most famous story about the Buddha's birth tells how he was born in a wood when his mother, Queen Maya, was on her way to visit her parents. It was a May night and the moon was full. Many strange events took place at the time of the baby's birth. The earth shook and two streams of water flowed from the sky. The trees in the wood blossomed. Blind people were able to see and lame people found that they could walk.

Seven days after her son's birth, Queen Maya died. The baby was brought up by his aunt in his father's luxurious palace.

Bodh Gaya ▼

Thousands of pilgrims visit Bodh Gaya every year. They can see a bodhi tree said to be descended from the tree that the Buddha was sitting under when he gained Enlightenment. They also visit the Mahabodhi Temple (below) to meditate and make offerings.

Sarnath ▲

This is the Dhamekh Stupa in Sarnath. People believe it marks the spot where the Buddha first explained his teaching after his Enlightenment. Pilgrims walk around the stupa three times, once for each of the Three Jewels (the Buddha, the Dharma, and the Sangha).

Tibetan Pilgrims ▶

Sacred places for Tibetans include temples, monasteries, and the Dalai Lama's palaces. The pilgrim in the photograph is standing in front of the Jokhang Temple in Lhasa. She is about to lie face down (prostrate) as part of her worship.

In May, the month of the Buddha's birthday, many pilgrims journey to Lhasa to visit the sacred places. They follow three special routes. One goes around the city. The others run inside and outside the Jokhang Temple.

WHAT ARE THE MAIN BUDDHIST FESTIVALS?

The most important Buddhist festivals celebrate events in the life of the Buddha, such as his birth and Enlightenment. They are held on full moon days, since tradition says this is when the events took place. The main festivals are marked by all groups of Buddhists, but the way they are celebrated differs from country to country.

Festival of the Sacred Tooth ▶

A tooth that is said to have belonged to the Buddha is kept in a temple near Kandy in Sri Lanka. On the night of the August full moon, it is carried through the town inside a miniature golden stupa, on the back of an elephant. Fire eaters, dancers, and drummers join in the magnificent procession.

KATHINA

In Thailand, a festival is held in November to celebrate the end of the rainy season. People go to their local monastery and give gifts to the monks to thank them for their work throughout the year. New robes are an especially important gift.

◀ Wesak

The children on the left are giving flowers to their parents to celebrate Wesak. This is when Theravada Buddhists remember the birth, Enlightenment, and death of the Buddha. It is celebrated on the day of the full moon in May and it is a very joyful festival. People visit the temple and decorate their homes with lanterns and flowers. They also send Wesak cards to their friends.

Loi Kratong ▼

Loi Kratong is the Thai festival of light. On the night of the November full moon, people place lamps made of leaves and candles in the rivers. The lamps are thought to carry away bad luck as they float away.

A lamp floating on the river for Loi Kratong

Hana Matsuri ▶

Japanese Buddhists celebrate the birth of the Buddha on April 8th, at a festival called Hana Matsuri. The children on the right are lining up to visit the temple. There, they will pour scented tea over a statue of the baby Buddha. This is a reminder of the two streams of water that were said to have poured from the sky to wash him when he was born (see page 34).

WHAT ARE THE MOST IMPORTANT TIMES IN A BUDDHIST'S LIFE?

Buddhists mark the special events in their lives in different ways, depending on the country they live in and the form of Buddhism they follow. Theravada Buddhists often invite monks to

their home when a baby is born, to chant from the sacred texts. When the baby is a month old, it may be taken to the temple and given a name.

BECOMING A BUDDHIST

People may be born into Buddhist families or they choose to become Buddhists. They make a commitment to the Three Jewels by saying the following words:

I go to the Buddha for refuge.
I go to the Dharma for refuge.
I go to the Sangha for refuge.

◄ **Buddhist Weddings**
Buddhist couples often make binding promises to each other and invite their friends to witness this. The couple might exchange rings and have their hands joined with a silk scarf to symbolize their marriage. A monk or other senior Buddhist may read from the sacred texts and bless the couple.

◄ Joining a Monastery

The boy on the left is preparing to join a monastery in Burma. His head has been shaved and he is being dressed in a maroon robe. The shaved head and the robe are symbols to show that he has given up his life in the world outside. Monks wear different-colored robes in different countries. In Thailand, they wear orange-yellow robes, but in Tibet, they wear maroon and in Japan, they wear black.

At the ordination (joining) ceremony, the boy will promise to be faithful to the Three Jewels. He will also recite the Ten Precepts, which are the ten rules that monks have to follow (see page 30).

Western Buddhists ►

Members of a group called Friends of the Western Buddhist Order do not wear robes. Instead, they wear a white cloth called a *kesa* (right) around their shoulders. It is decorated with a design that represents the Three Jewels.

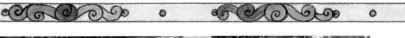

Kesa

Funeral Ceremony ►

The picture on the right shows a funeral ceremony. A monk leads the ceremony and the body may be buried or cremated. Buddhists believe that when a person dies, their consciousness flows on to a new human life. As people learn to act more kindly and wisely, their consciousness moves toward Enlightenment.

WHAT IS BUDDHIST ART LIKE?

When the Buddhist religion first began, pictures were never made of the Buddha himself. Instead, Buddhists used symbols to represent a part of the Buddha's life or teaching. Later, when Buddhism spread out of India, people began to make beautiful statues of the Buddha and of bodhisattvas.

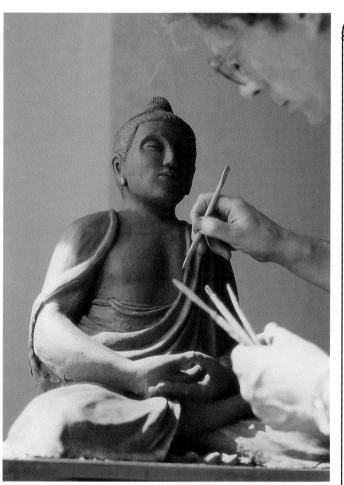

Special Signs ▲

Statues of the Buddha always include signs that show he was an extraordinary person. In this modern statue, for example, he has long earlobes. This shows he once wore heavy earrings. It is a sign that he belonged to a noble family.

MUDRAS

The position of the hands and fingers in statues of the Buddha and bodhisattvas have special meanings. These hand positions are called mudras.

This mudra represents the Buddha turning the Dharma wheel.

In this mudra, one hand is raised to show fearlessness and offer protection. The other shows generosity.

This mudra is described as "calling the earth to witness." It relates to the time when the Buddha became Enlightened.

This is the *mudra* of teaching.

Sand Mandala

The beautiful, complicated design on the left is made from colored sand. It is a mandala (see page 23) and the monks are making it for a festival. They are wearing masks so that their breath will not blow the sand out of place. It takes hours of practice and great skill to learn how to make designs like these.

Symbols of the Buddha ▶

The picture on the right shows the Buddha's footprints. This was one of the symbols used for the Buddha in early times. Other symbols were a wheel, a stupa, a lotus flower, a horse, a bodhi tree, and a royal umbrella held over an empty throne.

The Buddha's footprints

◀ Thangka Ceremony

These monks are unfolding a huge *thangka* painting at a ceremony in Tibet. A *thangka* is a sacred painting that shows scenes from Buddhist history, pictures of bodhisattvas, or the Wheel of Life. It is painted on cloth so that it can be rolled up and carried around.

DO BUDDHISTS LIKE STORIES?

Buddhists tell stories to help people to understand the Buddha's teaching. Many of the stories were first told by the Buddha himself and he was a clever storyteller.

The Jatakas are a collection of stories about the Buddha's past lives. They are part of the Pali Canon. In many of the tales, the Buddha takes the form of an animal, to teach the importance of qualities such as loving kindness, wisdom, patience, and generosity.

 PAST LIVES

These are some of the animal forms that the Buddha takes in the Jatakas.

Golden peacock

Hare

Golden stag

Lion

White elephant

White horse

The Story of the Lion and the Jackal
In this story from the Jatakas, the Buddha shows that one good turn deserves another.

In one of his past lives, the Buddha was born as a lion. He lived on a high mountain. The mountain was surrounded by water, but there was a small island of marshy land nearby. Rabbits and deer lived there.

One day, the lion saw a deer grazing on the island and rushed to snatch it in his jaws. But as he pounced, his feet became stuck in the marshy ground. He was trapped in the mud there for seven days.

On the seventh day, a jackal came by. He turned to run away when he saw the lion, but the lion begged the jackal to rescue him. So the jackal scooped away the mud and tugged at the lion until he was free.

By now, the lion was very hungry indeed. He killed a bull and asked the jackal to share the feast, to show how grateful he was for the jackal's help. Then he invited the jackal to come and live near him, so that he could protect the jackal and his family.

The two families lived happily side by side for a while. But then the lioness began to get jealous of the time the lion spent with the jackal's family. She suggested to the jackal's wife that it was time for the jackals to go.

The jackal's wife told her husband what the lioness had said. So one day, when the lion and the jackal were out hunting together, the jackal said that they would soon be leaving. The lion was surprised and upset. He wanted to know why the jackal was going, and soon, the whole story came out.

When the lion got home he reminded his wife of how the jackal had helped him when he was in trouble. "However small and lowly he is," said the lion, "that jackal saved my life. That makes him my friend, forever and ever." Now the lioness understood that one good turn deserves another, and from then on, the lions and the jackals lived together in peace.

GLOSSARY

alms Gifts of food, money, or other goods to monks, nuns, or the poor. Monks traditionally collect these gifts in an alms bowl.

bodhisattva A person who has achieved enlightenment but has chosen to be reborn instead of entering nirvana, in order to help other people to achieve enlightenment.

Buddha The word means "Awakened one" or "Enlightened one." Siddhartha Gautama, who founded the Buddhist religion, was known as "the Buddha" after his Enlightenment.

chants Words that are half sung, half spoken.

Dalai Lama The political leader of Tibet and the religious leader of the country's Buddhists.

Dharma The Buddha's teachings and the way people practice them in their daily lives.

Enlightenment The experience of deeply understanding the truth about how life really is and how you can be happy.

Five Precepts Five guidelines that Buddhists follow in their daily lives.

incense A substance that gives off a sweet, spicy smell when it is burned.

karma The teaching that actions have consequences. Kind actions lead to happiness; unkind actions lead to unhappiness.

meditate To sit quietly and focus your mind, sometimes using a word or picture, until you become totally calm and peaceful.

monastery A building where monks or nuns live, study, and worship together.

nirvana Enlightenment.

pagoda A building in China or Japan that contains sacred relics or writings.

Pali Canon The sacred books of Theravada Buddhists, written in the ancient language, Pali. They are believed to contain the words of the Buddha himself.

pilgrims People who make a journey to a holy place, such as a temple or shrine.

relics Objects that once belonged to a holy person, or even a part of their body. For example, the Buddha's tooth is a relic kept in Kandy, Sri Lanka.

requisites Items that are essential to perform a job, or for daily life.

sacred Holy; devoted to a god or goddess or the Buddha; or used for a religious purpose.

Sangha This word can mean the community of monks and nuns, or it can include all Buddhists.

scroll Writing on a long piece of paper or other material. It has to be unrolled to read it.

shrine A place where images of the Buddha or bodhisattvas are kept and honored. This might be in the home or in a temple.

stupa A building that contains sacred relics or writings, or marks a place where a special event in Buddhist history took place.

temple A building where Buddhists worship.

Three Jewels The Buddha, his teachings (Dharma), and the Buddhist community (Sangha), which Buddhists take as their guides in life.

Zen Buddhism A form of Mahayana Buddhism followed mainly in China and Japan. Zen Buddhists emphasize meditation as a path to Enlightenment.

FURTHER READING

A Pebble For Your Pocket
by Nhat Nanh
(Plum Blossom Books, 2002)

Atlas of World Faiths: Buddhism
by Anita Ganeri
(Smart Apple Media, 2007)

World Religions: Buddhism
by Don Nardo
(Compass Point Books, 2009)

INDEX

WEB SITES

Due to the changing nature of Internet links, Rosen Publishing
has developed an online list of Web sites related to the subject
of this book. This site is updated regularly. Please use this link
to access this list: http://www.rosenlinks.com/wrel/budd